Animal Boxing Stars

BY REBECCA BARONE

Published by The Child's World®
1980 Lookout Drive • Mankato, MN 56003-1705
800-599-READ • www.childsworld.com

Photographs ©: Chris Howey/Shutterstock Images, cover, 1; jspix/
ImageBroker RM/Glow Images, 5; Paolo Bona/Shutterstock
Images, 6; Dan Grossi/AP Images, 7; Nagel Photography/
Shutterstock Images, 9, 20–21; Jean-Paul Ferrero/AUSCAPE/
Auscape International Pty Ltd/Alamy, 10; Picture Partners/
iStockphoto, 11; Franco Banfi/NHPA/Photoshot/Newscom, 13;
Andrea Izzotti/Shutterstock Images, 14, 20; Shutterstock Images,
17, 21; Juniors Bildarchiv GmbH/Alamy, 18

ISBN 9781503820371
LCCN 2016960507

Printed in the United States of America
PA02341

ABOUT THE AUTHOR

Rebecca Barone has a degree in English and several degrees in mechanical engineering. In her career, Rebecca has worked in the automotive industry, has studied injury biomechanics for the NFL, and has been a scientist at the Air Force Research Laboratories. She lives in Dayton, Ohio, with her husband and son.

Contents

CHAPTER 1

Boxing Stars . . . 4

CHAPTER 2

Double-Punch Knockouts . . . 8

CHAPTER 3

Fighting with Poisonous Jabs . . . 12

CHAPTER 4

The Hardest Hitter . . . 16

CHAPTER 5

The Award Ceremony . . . 20

Glossary . . . 22

To Learn More . . . 23

Index . . . 24

Boxing Stars

The animal world is filled with claws, fists, and powerful limbs. For some animals, being a good fighter is the only way to survive.

In the wild, animals fight to get food, defend themselves, and become the leader of a pack. To win a fight, an animal must be strong and fast. Strong animals can punch and kick to hurt and kill other animals. Fast animals can attack quickly and run away. Some animals have special skills that help them fight. This is like having a weapon in addition to just hands and feet.

Humans also fight in a sport called boxing. Boxing is one of the oldest sports in the world. It was even a sport in the Olympics in ancient Greece.

Boxing isn't a sport for animals—
it's a way to survive.

Unlike animal boxers, human boxers fight in a ring with boxing gloves and a helmet.

In boxing, athletes score points by hitting an opponent with their fists. Judges award points based on how often an athlete punches his or her opponent. Star human boxers have to be strong and fast, just like animals.

Muhammad Ali is considered one of the greatest boxers of all time. He was known for his speed.

If this were a competition, which animal would win in a boxing match? To help us decide which is the greatest animal boxer, we will answer three questions: How does the animal punch or kick? Can the animal move fast? Does the animal have other defenses to help in a fight?

At the end, we'll award gold, silver, and bronze medals to our champions!

ATHLETE PROFILE

NAME: Muhammad Ali

BORN: January 17, 1942, in Louisville, Kentucky

HEIGHT: 6.25 feet (191 cm)

WEIGHT: Ranged from 188 to 236 pounds (85 to 107 kg)

SIGNATURE MOVE: Fast punches and fast feet

CHAPTER 2

Double-Punch Knockouts

Red kangaroos are found in Australia. These **marsupials** have short forelegs and large, muscular hind limbs. They also have a very strong tail. How do strong limbs and a strong tail help the kangaroo fight?

In a fight, a red kangaroo will lean back on its tail and kick out with both hind limbs at the same time. Imagine getting hit with two punches at once. This is a strong move that will hurt a predator. This move can break bones of other animals, and even kill.

ANIMAL PROFILE
NAME: Red Kangaroo
HEIGHT: 3.25 to 5.25 feet (99 to 160 cm)
TAIL LENGTH: 3 to 3.6 feet (0.9 to 1.1 m)
WEIGHT: Up to 200 pounds (91 kg)
SIGNATURE MOVE: Hind leg jab

There are more kangaroos than humans in Australia!

Red kangaroos use their strong tail to help them balance during a fight.

Female red kangaroos keep joeys, or baby kangaroos, in a pouch on their stomach.

Red kangaroos can also move very fast by jumping from place to place. They jump using their strong hind limbs. Some red kangaroos can jump up to 35 miles per hour (56 km/h).

These kangaroos eat grass and leaves. They live together in packs. The red kangaroo will stomp its foot when it senses danger. This warns other animals.

With such powerful hind limbs and fast jumping, kangaroos are fierce boxers.

Fun Fact

The red kangaroo is the largest marsupial in the world.

CHAPTER 3

Fighting with Poisonous Jabs

Boxer crabs, also known as pom-pom crabs, live in the Pacific and Indian Oceans. These crabs are very small. They are rare to see. The biggest boxer crabs are only half an inch (1.3 cm) wide. Can such a small animal be a good fighter?

In a fight, boxer crabs get help from sea anemones. Each boxer crab carries poisonous sea anemones in its front claws. When the boxer crab attacks, it hits the other animal with the sea anemones.

ANIMAL PROFILE
NAME: Boxer Crab
LENGTH: Up to half an inch (1.3 cm)
WEIGHT: Unknown
SIGNATURE MOVE: Jab and hook with a poisonous sea anemone

Boxer crabs are nicknamed "pom-pom crabs" because when they hold the sea anemones in their hands they look like cheerleaders.

If needed, boxer crabs can regenerate, or regrow, a lost limb.

The sea anemones are special weapons that help this small animal win. Boxer crabs can also kick when fighting other boxer crabs.

Boxer crabs live in coral and sand. The shells of boxer crabs are pink, yellow, and brown. These colors help **camouflage** the boxer crab. Hiding through camouflage is another way that the boxer crab defends itself.

Boxer crabs are often kept as pets. In captivity, boxer crabs eat small pieces of squid and shrimp.

They may be small, but fighting with poisonous sea anemones makes these boxer crabs good fighters.

Fun Fact

Boxer crabs help sea anemones in return by moving them to new sources of food.

CHAPTER 4

The Hardest Hitter

There are almost 6,000 kinds of lizards in the world. Lizards are found on every continent except for Antarctica. The spiny-tailed lizard lives in North Africa and the Middle East. It can be found on rocky hills.

The thick tail of the spiny-tailed lizard is covered in pointed **armor**. The lizard can use this tail as a club. The spiny-tailed lizard may also bite if it feels threatened, although this is rare.

ANIMAL PROFILE
NAME: Spiny-Tailed Lizard
LENGTH: 10 to 18 inches (25 to 46 cm)
WEIGHT: 0.3 to 0.9 pounds (0.1 to 0.4 kg)
SIGNATURE MOVE: Using tail as a club to hit opponents

The Egyptian spiny-tailed lizard is also called the dhub lizard in the Middle East.

The spiny-tailed lizard also uses its tail as a defense against predators. Anything that bites down on the spiky tail would be in pain.

The spiny-tailed lizard can sprint but only for short distances. When threatened, the lizard runs headfirst into its **burrow**. It expands its body to fill the entrance. Humans can puff out their cheeks, and this is similar to what the spiny-tailed lizard does to its whole body!

The spiny-tailed lizard mostly eats plants. It also eats lentils. Lentils are small dried legumes. The spiny-tailed lizard rarely drinks water. Instead, it gets water from the plants it eats. This lizard spends almost all day outside its burrow during the summer. Many people keep spiny-tailed lizards as pets.

With a strong, pointed tail, this lizard is a good fighter.

Fun Fact

This lizard can change color according to body temperature.

CHAPTER 5

The Award Ceremony

GOLD MEDAL
Boxer Crab

The gold medal goes to the boxer crab! Fighting with poisonous sea anemones gives the boxer crab an advantage. The red kangaroo wins the silver medal. The bronze medal goes to the spiny-tailed lizard. Strength, speed, and special moves are just some of the ways these animals are truly stars! Congratulations to all the winners!

BRONZE MEDAL
Spiny-Tailed Lizard

SILVER MEDAL
Red Kangaroo

Glossary

armor (AR-mer) Armor is clothing or covering used to protect the body during battle. The hard spikes on the tail of the spiny-tailed lizard act as armor.

burrow (BUR-oh) A burrow is a hole or tunnel in the ground that an animal uses for a home. Spiny-tailed lizards live in burrows.

camouflage (KAM-uh-flazh) To camouflage is to hide an animal or person by making them look like the things around them. Boxer crabs are hard to see, because their shell is camouflaged with the coral.

marsupials (mar-SOO-pee-uls) Marsupials are mammals that carry their babies in a pouch on their stomachs. Red kangaroos are marsupials that hop on two legs.

To Learn More

In the Library

Bishop, Nic. *Lizards*. New York, NY: Scholastic, 2010.

Gish, Melissa. *Crabs*. Mankato, MN: Creative Education/Creative Paperbacks, 2016.

Lunis, Natalie. *Red Kangaroo: The World's Largest Marsupial*. New York, NY: Bearport, 2010.

On the Web

Visit our Web site for links about animals that box: **childsworld.com/links**

Note to Parents, Teachers, and Librarians: We routinely verify our Web links to make sure they are safe and active sites. So encourage your readers to check them out!

Index

Ali, Muhammad, 6–7
ancient Greece, 4
Australia, 8

boxer crabs, 12, 14, 21

Indian Ocean, 12

Middle East, 16

North Africa, 16

Pacific Ocean, 12

red kangaroo, 8, 10, 21

sea anemones, 12, 14, 21
spiny-tailed lizard, 16, 19, 21